ABANDONED NORTHWEST FLORIDA

KIM HILL

AMERICA THROUGH TIME®
ADDING COLOR TO AMERICAN HISTORY

This book is dedicated to all the explorers out there. The ones who see what others would ignore. The ones who use their imagination to create stories behind every abandoned building, boat, or other type of forgotten area.

America Through Time is an imprint of Fonthill Media LLC
www.through-time.com
office@through-time.com

Published by Arcadia Publishing by arrangement with Fonthill Media LLC
For all general information, please contact Arcadia Publishing:
Telephone: 843-853-2070
Fax: 843-853-0044
E-mail: sales@arcadiapublishing.com
For customer service and orders:
Toll-Free 1-888-313-2665

www.arcadiapublishing.com

First published 2020

ISBN 978-1-63499-214-5

Typeset in Trade Gothic 10pt on 15pt
Printed and bound in England

CONTENTS

ABOUT THE AUTHOR

Kim Hill is a freelance writer, author, website designer, painter, award-winning photographer, and overall Jill-of-All-Trades that lives in sunny, and often stormy, Florida—where there's always something happening in the news. Shauna Klein is her horror author pen name and she has contributed to books under her given name.

Kim has two degrees in criminology and loves all-things crime and horror related. She is also an advocate for SkinCancer.net where she helps educate others on what to expect when dealing with skin cancer.

Kim recently had three of her photographs selected for the Clio Art Fair in Chelsea, NYC, and is currently working on a horror anthology. She is thankful she survived Hurricane Michael and can start to piece her life back together and see her beautiful city rebuild.

INTRODUCTION

Commonly referred to as the Panhandle, Northwest Florida is an estimated 200-mile-long strip of land that borders Alabama, Georgia, and the Gulf of Mexico.

Part of Northwest Florida includes Pensacola, which was the first European settlement in United States. It was settled by the Spanish in 1559 and was the state capital up until 1821. After settlers from Georgia and Alabama made their way to Northwest Florida, it became a predominately rural area until after WWII.

What started as an area with fishing, farming, and mills soon became an area with a military presence. It was in 1935 that the largest military installation in the United States was built in the Ft. Walton Beach area.

Because of the sugar white sands and emerald clear waters, Northwest Florida has become a major tourist destination. Whether it's spring breakers during the months around March, families in the summer, or snowbirds in the winter—the Panhandle is a highly sought-after place to be.

This doesn't mean everything is picture perfect and there aren't plenty of areas for urban exploration. In fact, one of the places is steeped in dark history. Others are simply forgotten or left behind by fleeing homeowners or defunct businesses.

Areas of Northwest Florida were hit by Hurricane Michael in October 2018. This was the strongest hurricane to ever hit the panhandle, the third-most intense Atlantic hurricane to make landfall in the United States in terms of pressure, and the strongest Atlantic hurricane in wind speeds to make landfall in the United States since Hurricane Andrew. In addition, it was the fourth strongest hurricane in the recorded history of the United States by wind speed.

What does this have to do with abandoned buildings? There are many more now. Thousands of buildings sit empty, damaged, or abandoned. None of these photos were taken after the storm—that's for another day.

1

BIG BEND JAI ALAI

Located just 25 miles from Tallahassee is the former Big Bend Jai Alai fronton. The Jai Alai fronton opened in 1978, but had problems from the beginning. Almost right after it opened, the owner died of a heart attack. His estate, valued at $22 million, was disputed by almost everyone—business associates, relatives, and his heirs all wanted a piece of the pie. This sat in court for around thirteen years, and while nothing was ever proven, there were crazy allegations about hidden gold and gems, as well as trickery and injustice.

While Jai Alai was hugely popular around the globe and a big success specifically in Miami, it didn't take off as much in Northwest Florida. After a player strike in 1988, Jai Alai was destined to start sliding into obscurity.

The last season of Big Bend Jai Alai was in 1990. There were plans to convert the building into a dog racing track, casino, etc., but all these plans fell through. Now, the building has sat empty for almost thirty years.

Surprisingly, there is still paperwork, blueprints, stuffed animals, and up until recently—even liquor bottles still full—inside the building. It's rife with colorful graffiti and one only must point a flashlight upwards to see the bat infestation.

All the doors and windows are missing their glass. It's a creepy place where it's best to skip going upstairs just in case the flooring isn't safe. Right now, it's a staging area for Hurricane Michael workers, which helps it be just a little less desolate.

Big Bend Jai Alai

Old staircase for Big Bend Jai Alai

Bathroom in Big Bend Jai Alai

Main viewing area of Big Bend Jai Alai

The Club Room

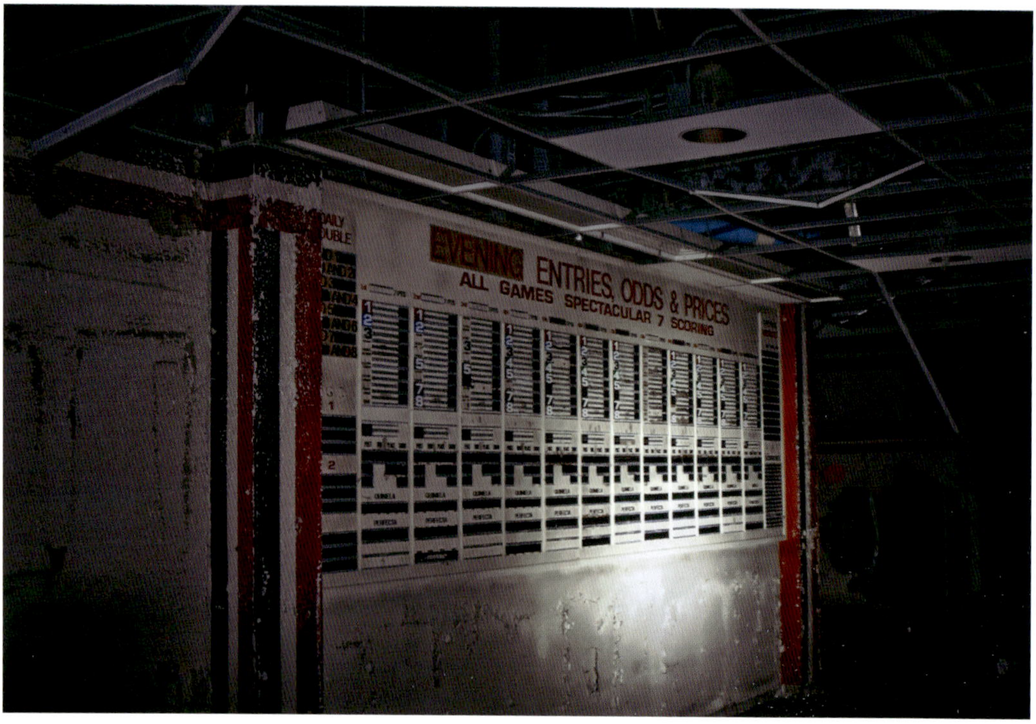

Evening entries, odds, and prices board

An old board menu

Graffiti

Storage room

More graffiti in the entrance area

2

PET CEMETERIES

Neither one of these pet cemeteries had any information that could be found about their demise. There are still graves of pets in the back and those look well-kept. Do the pet owners do the upkeep? Surely the owners of at least one of the pet cemeteries has moved on, judging by the look of Poodle-A-Rama's main building. Regardless, both have quite a story to tell.

The Poodle-A-Rama cemetery is in Panama City, Florida. It was well-kept, all but the main building where the funerals were held. After Hurricane Michael, the cemetery is inaccessible, with felled trees throughout the grounds.

Pet Haven Cemetery is in Northwest Pensacola. While it is seemingly abandoned, the grounds have been maintained throughout the years. Word has it that the land has been sold and the pet cemetery will become something else. What will happen to the pets that are buried there?

Pet cemetery

Poodle-A-Rama cemetery

Above: Poodle-A-Rama main building

Right: Pamphlet for pet memorials

Inside the pet cemetery church

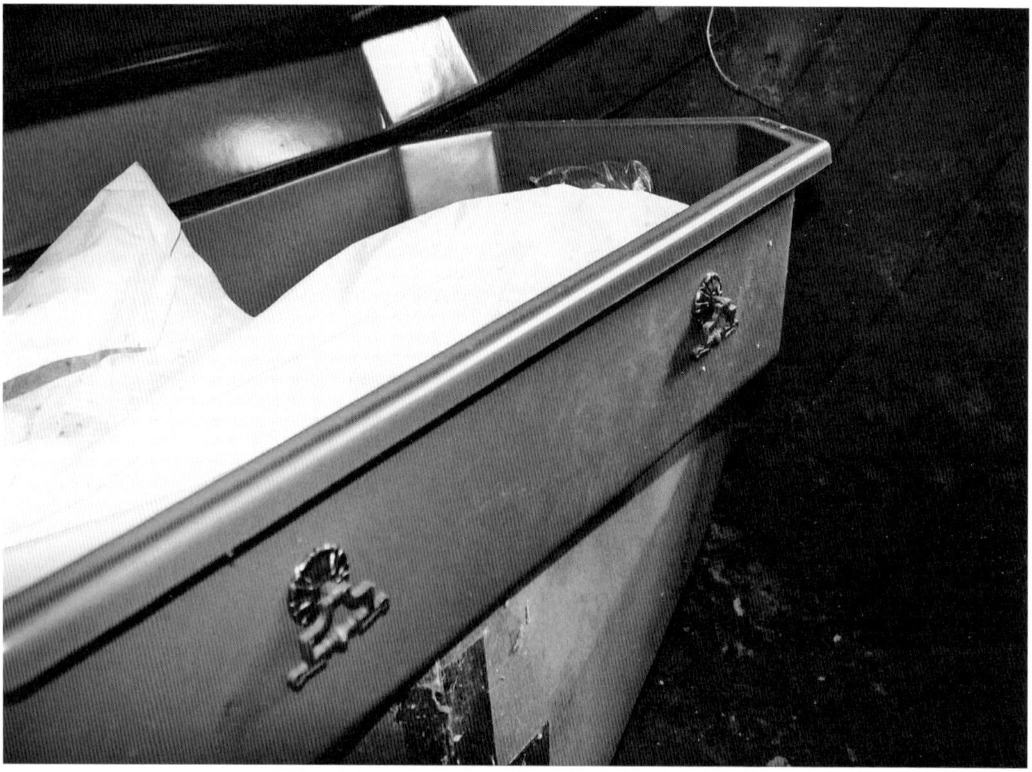

An old empty casket

More caskets and supplies

Inside the church

Above: Pet Haven Cemetery [*Andy Hudson*]

Left: A memorial at Pet Haven courtesy of Andy Hudson

3

PLANES, TRAINS, AND AUTOMOBILES

Eglin Reservation Crash

On January 25, 1968, a C-123K Provider (c/n 20179) of the 4408th Combat Crew Training Squadron, 4410th Combat Crew Training Wing crashed on approach to Duke Field, the airframe coming down on the Eglin reservation just 1/2 mile from the runway threshold. According to USAF Serials by Joe Baugher, it started out life as a C-123B-12-FA and was converted to C-123K-12-FA.

The men killed in the crash were identified as Maj. Donald R. Tomlinson, Fort Walton Beach, Fla.; SSgt. James H. Jefferies, Destin, Fla.; Lt. Francis G. Guidry, Ville Platte, La.; and Lt. Stanley R. Armstrong from Mesa, Arizona.

According to an Air Force spokesman, four witnesses in the control tower reported that the plane was circling the field making practice landings. The plane was in a landing pattern when it suddenly turned off as it approached the runway and never came out of the turn.

The aircraft is on the Eglin AFB Reservation, but not physically on the base. A recreational permit is needed from the Jackson Guard to get out to the aircraft. This aircraft is mistakenly referred to as the Duke Field C-130 crash site by various sites on the internet.

Eglin Reservation Crash [*Michael C. Bernhardt*]

Eglin Reservation Crash [*Michael C. Bernhardt*]

Eglin Reservation Crash [*Michael C. Bernhardt*]

Eglin Reservation Crash [*Michael C. Bernhardt*]

The Apalachicola & Northern Railroad

The Apalachicola & Northern Railroad's (reporting mark: AN) former headquarters feature an abandoned shop area located in Port St. Joe, Florida. It was started in 1903 and it was in operation up until the 80s when the rail-served industry moved out of Port St. Joe. It ran from the Gulf Coast to the Georgia border with approximately 100 miles of rail. It fell into bankruptcy several times and had several owners, including DuPont. The 1940s also saw the railroad replacing its steam power for much more modern diesel. In 1996, DuPont sold the mill property. After their largest company closed its doors, it was renamed as the AN Railway. Yet, it still faced difficulty remaining open.

Today, the Apalachicola & Northern Railroad has a short line of operation from Hosford, Florida, to Chattahoochee, Florida. The rest is now defunct—just like the shops you see here at its former headquarters.

Apalachicola & Northern Railroad

Apalachicola & Northern Railroad

Pat Harvey's Abandoned Cars

Many of the abandoned cars and trucks you'll see are simply just left along the road. But a little bit south of Tallahassee lies a vintage Ford graveyard. These trucks fill up their resting place with memories and nostalgia.

The trucks are owned by Pat Harvey. Harvey's farm is near the site where he lined up each vehicle by its production date. For Harvey, they're filled with family memories, he told local television station WFSU in 2012. "That's the one I took my driver's test in, and got my driver's license," he said, about a 1959 model. One of the station wagons he used to pick up dates."

The elements (and theft) have not treated the vehicles well. There are broken windows, rust, corrosion, and items stolen off the cars. Mother Nature has grown her plants throughout.

There are always transportation vehicles at-random. They have no known story, but are just as intriguing.

An old car sits at Pat Harvey's farm

Interior of an old car

Pat Harvey's old cars almost look like toys from a child

More abandoned cars

Above left: Another of Pat Harvey's cars

Above right: An old neglected car near heading towards Tallahassee

Above: An abandoned Air Force plane

Opposite above: Old truck

Opposite below: An old train car

8846

4

A NIGHTMARE HISTORY AT DOZIER SCHOOL FOR BOYS

West of Tallahassee are the remains of the Dozier School for Boys. It has been known by many names, including the Florida State Reform School, opened in 1900. There are 1,400 acres that make up the abandoned school and people still keep secrets of what went on there.

Throughout the school's history, it was known for its treatment of the boys who were sent there. The school was operated by the state of Florida in the town of Marianna from January 1, 1900, to June 30, 2011, when it closed for good.

Boys were sent there for all kinds of infractions—even minor ones like smoking or truancy. During its history, there were rumors of rape, torture, beatings, and even murder. While the school had been investigated periodically, there were always promises of improvement or changes in leadership that ensured it remained open. That is, until 2011, when it was closed permanently after multiple investigations.

Known as the "White House Boys," there have been over 300 men who have come forward with stories of their time at Dozier in the 1950s and 1960s. There were violent beatings, torture, and more. Around eighty-one boys died there.

State investigators said that using school records, they were able to identify 31 former students interred in the school cemetery. Records show 50 other boys also died at the school, with no indication of where most are buried.

Not only were there multiple deaths throughout the years, there were unmarked graves inside and outside of the cemetery boundaries. With over 100 deaths that were documented, there were fifty-five unmarked graves in the woods or brush areas outside of the cemetery boundaries.

Investigations started in 2008, led by Florida Governor Charlie Crist. The FDLE conducted over 100 interviews of family members, former students, and staff members. There was no solid evidence of deaths or concealment of deaths during the time period of the "White House Boys."

In January 2010, the Department of Law Enforcement released its findings:

> This investigation included over one hundred interviews of former students, family of former students, and former staff members of the school. The interviews confirmed that in addition to the implementation of the Individual Rating System, school administrators used corporal punishment as a tool to encourage obedience. The interviews revealed little disagreement about the way in which corporal punishment was administered. The former students were consistent in that punishment was administered by school administrators and adult staff witnesses in the building referred to as the White House. The former students were consistent in stating that a wooden paddle or leather strap was the implement used for administering punishment. The area of disagreement among former students was the number of spankings administered and their severity. Although some former students stated that they were "beaten" to the point that the skin of their buttocks blistered and bled profusely, there was little to no evidence of visible residual scarring. A secondary disagreement was the former students' perceptions of the punishment process. Some former students stated that their spankings caused them no psychological harm and that they learned from their mistakes, while others stated that, mentally, they suffered greatly as a result and still do so to this day.
>
> Some reports by former students stated that in addition to corporal punishment, they were also subjected to sexual abuse at the hands of former staff members or other students. With the passage of over fifty years, no tangible physical evidence was found to either support or refute the allegations of physical or sexual abuse.

Yet in 2012, the University of South Florida, led by Dr. Erin Kimmerle, a forensic scientist, explored the campus with biologists, anthropologists, and archaeologists. By December of that same year, they located fifty-five graves. Since 100 graves were documented, they felt they had found a secondary cemetery. In 2013, an injunction was granted to excavate, exhume, and examine the bodies buried in those graves since there were no records of the deaths, who they were, or what happened.

> In January 2014, the USF team issued their final report. They had made a total of seven DNA matches and 14 presumptive identifications from the 51 remains found at the site. A total of 55 burials were identified, but only 13 were made within the cemetery grounds. Others were outside, 13 of the graves were located in the school's cemetery and "the rest of the graves were outside ..."in the woods, including under a roadway, brush, and a large mulberry tree." While they had documented 98 deaths at the site,

Dozier School for Boys church

Through the fence at Dozier

Above left: Walkway to Dozier

Above right: Another view of the walkway

Across the street from Dozier—part of the school, but not fenced in

Above: Across from Dozier

Left: The fencing at Dozier
[*Bruce Benedict*]

they were unable to identify any more burials on the grounds. Some bodies may have been sent home to students' families. The USF team will continue to work with other organizations and families on DNA and other means of identification of the remains that were found. They created computer facial approximations from remains to help with identification. A number of families, including the Glen Varnadoe family, have filed requests to have the remains of their children or relatives repatriated.

Today, the Dozier School for Boys stands empty. Its grounds are well-kept, it is surrounded by barbed wire fencing, and security stands at the gate. No one is allowed inside to take pictures and you're lucky if security doesn't run you off from the entire area. We were lucky to find a security guard who was friendly and allowed us to take pictures as long as they were from the outside. If I had a drone, I would have gone back to see what else I could photograph, although surely that's not exactly something that they allow.

Inside of Dozier School for Boys

Across from Dozier, but part of the campus

Across from Dozier

Across from the school

More of Dozier from across the street

Dozier campus buildings

Church on Dozier's campus

Dozier [*Mike Woodfin*]

5

BRIDGES AND BOATS

Being on the coast, you'll always find boats and bridges and some of the abandoned ones have the most interesting stories.

BELLAMY BRIDGE

Bellamy Bridge is a historic bridge located in Marianna, Florida. What is one of the oldest bridges in Florida and the oldest of its type is now a historic site with a rich background that includes tales of a haunting.

The History of Bellamy Bridge

Bellamy Bridge is a steel frame bridge that was built in 1914. It is located on the upper part of the Chipola River and was used as a crossing point for hundreds of years. In fact, it was recorded to have been used by Marcos Delgado, a Spanish explorer, as far back as 1686. While there is no proof, according to the records, this is the area he and his men were in and it is the only area that fits the description according to geographical information.

In 1851, a wooden bridge was erected, called Bellamy's Bridge. However, the elements ruined that bridge, and another was put in its place in 1872. After two years, a major flood happened on the Chipola River and that bridge was swept away. In 1874, a third bridge was built but was replaced with the bridge that stands today, in 1914. It is not only the oldest bridge in Florida of steel framing but is one of the ten oldest bridges of any kind in the entire state.

This bridge was used up until 1963 when the County Road 163 was built and has since fallen into disrepair. While the steel frame stands tall, the wooden flooring planks have since fallen into Chipola River.

Bellamy Bridge

Side view of Bellamy Bridge

The Haunting of Bellamy Bridge

What is particularly unique about Bellamy Bridge is that it is part of one of the most well-known haunted areas in Florida. The ghost story involves an eighteen-year-old by the name of Elizabeth Jane Croom Bellamy. The legend is quite different from the truth, but both are amazing stories.

Legend has it that Elizabeth married her true love, Dr. Samuel Bellamy. They supposedly married in a rose garden on the grounds of a mansion he had built for her. This mansion was on the site where the Bellamy Bridge is located and has since been long gone. After the beautiful ceremony, she retired to her room to rest and supposedly caught her wedding dress on fire by knocking over a candelabra that was lit. She ran down the stairs on fire much to the shock of her wedding guests and while they tried to save her, she died a few days later. Supposedly her last words to her new husband were during her wedding vows where she said, ""I will love you always and forever. Never will I leave you."

After the distraught husband committed suicide fifteen years later, she came back to find him and still shows up at the Bellamy Bridge.

However, the true story is quite another tale. While the people are real, the true story is that Elizabeth did die in Florida but not at her wedding. Her wedding wasn't even in Florida, but rather North Carolina.

Elizabeth was married at fifteen and gave birth to a son two years later. When she was just eighteen, she got malaria and died in May of 1837. There is a newspaper obituary that has the record of her death. Unfortunately, the part about her husband committing suicide is true. Samuel killed himself with a straight razor and requested before his death to be buried by his bride. Since suicide victims were not buried in church cemeteries, Samuel was buried in an unmarked grave in Chattahoochee.

As far back as 1890, there have been reported sightings of Elizabeth's ghost around the Bellamy Bridge. Back then she was called "The Lady of Bellamy Bridge." Coincidentally, there are at least three other ghost tales surrounding this bridge including a man who murdered his wife, then committed suicide, and a moonshiner who was murdered there.

While Bellamy Bridge still stands, it sits at a half mile walk into the woods. There is nothing else around but Mother Nature. However, there is a walking trail that is open to the public that was put into place by Northwest Florida Water Management District, Jackson County Parks & Recycling, and the Friends of Bellamy Bridge. This trail allows visitors to park in a public parking area and walk down the trail to the bridge. There are benches along the trail for convenience and at the bridge site, there are signs telling the history of the site, including the ghost story.

The park is only open during daylight hours, but there are tours that can be taken at night by contacting the Bellamy Bridge Organization.

Abandoned Boats

Along the Gulf Coast, banks are dotted with abandoned boats. Some are eventually found and retrieved by their owners, while others sit and eventually become rotted and forever grounded. Regardless of how they are eventually taken care of, they make for interesting photos and even more interesting tales of where they came from.

Abandoned boat

Neglected boat in Apalachicola

Washed up sailboat near Inlet Beach

Last Echo

Lost sailboat

Abandoned boats [*Steven Bauer*]

[*Steven Bauer*]

[*Steven Bauer*]

Last Echo

The Star Dancer

Abandoned dock

Sailboat near Grayton Beach

Abandoned boat [*Steven Bauer*]

[*Steven Bauer*]

[*Steven Bauer*]

[*Steven Bauer*]

[*Steven Bauer*]

6

HAMPTON SPRINGS

Back in the late 1800s, Taylor County resident, Joe Hamilton, was led to a sulfur-rich spring by Indians of the area. Hamilton's wife suffered from rheumatism and the springs seemed to ease her pain. Hamilton then purchased a government grant to the area. What started out as that plot of land became a partnership between Benjamin W. and Joseph L. Hampton, then businessman J. W. Oglesby joined to create the Hampton Springs Hotel.

This hotel resort was known for the healing powers of the sulfur baths and springs. It was a retreat for the wealthy and included a ballroom, casino, stables, tennis courts, a covered pool, an outdoor dance pavilion, and elaborate gardens and fountains. Along with the hotel, there was a bottling plant. There, bottles of the healing water were shipped out to customers all over the country. The grounds also featured a hunting lodge and fishing lodge—both private.

In 1954, the hotel caught fire and burned to the ground. The area was left to become ruins that are still visible today. In fact, the area is a park now that features picnic areas and hiking trails. This is conflicting, because on one hand, visitors will always get to see the grounds as long as the park controls them. However, it also makes it a place that just anyone can visit and photograph. That makes it feel just a little less abandoned. However, the story behind the springs and hotel are so interesting, it's well-worth the visit.

Interestingly, according to Desolation Florida:

> The springs have been entirely enclosed in these concrete pools. Despite the algae growing in the pool, the water flowing from the spring (coming up from that dark hole in the center) is crystal clear—although it has a strong sulfur smell!

Hampton Springs [*Ebyabe*]

Opposite above: Hampton Springs [*Michael Rivera*]

Opposite below: Hampton Springs [*Ebyabe*]

7

BUILDINGS FROM THE PAST (AND OTHER ODDITIES)

Northwest Florida has no shortage of random abandoned buildings. Many have a history that is untapped, and you never know what you'll find—especially in some of the smaller towns.

Abandoned silos

Abandoned warehouse

Old YMCA in Destin

Old YMCA in Destin [*Bruce Benedict*]

Old YMCA in Destin

Old YMCA in Destin

Old YMCA in Destin

Abandoned warehouse

Perry Motor Lodge sign

Old Sky Ride in Panama City Beach

Old Sky Ride in Panama City Beach

Overgrown and left to rust

Old lodge by the train tracks

More of the old lodge

Part of the amusement park that was once in Pier Park

Seafood processing building in Apalachicola

Under the dock of the seafood processing building in Apalachicola

Seafood processing building in Apalachicola

Seafood processing building in Apalachicola

Dock of the seafood processing building in Apalachicola

Old building in Cottondale

Old repair shop in Callaway

Inside of the repair shop [*Richard Hill*]

Inside the repair shop [*Richard Hill*]

Old Copacabana

Copacabana

Old Motel

Deserted Motel

Old Motel

Old Motel

Part of the Copacabana

Old building

Old building

Hidden in the woods

Almost overgrown completely

Abandoned elementary school

Entrance to an old park near Gulf Breeze

Forgotten trailers

Leftover restaurant

Above: Barbecue sauce still sits in the restaurant

Right: Old shack

8

FORGOTTEN NEIGHBORHOODS AND ABANDONED HOMES

No one knows why some homes are abandoned and new residential developments sit empty. Much of it could be to finances falling through. That's certainly not true in all cases—just some. Sometimes, families move and the homes seem to fall through the cracks, sitting empty for what seems like eternity, or at least until they rot away or fall in.

Country home

Abandoned beach home courtesy of Bruce Benedict

Two for the price of one

Claimed by a fire

Let the sky in

Once a nice swim

Country manor courtesy of Mike Woodfin

Abandoned home sits in front of luxury home courtesy of Bruce Benedict

Beach home left behind courtesy of Bruce Benedict

Hidden in plain sight

Lost in the woods

Uninhabitable home near Freeport

House in the woods near Freeport

Old home left behind

Another view of the old home

Abandoned home in Panama City

Neglected home

Even the birds have no home

Eden

Eden's clubhouse

The pool at Eden is fairly clear

A quiet place to sit at Eden

View from the woods at Eden

Kitt's Tower

Kitt's Tower

Morningside entrance

BIBLIOGRAPHY

Allen, G. "Florida's Dozier School For Boys: A True Horror Story," *NPR,* www.npr.org/2012/10/15/162941770/floridas-dozier-school-for-boys-a-true-horror-story, October 2012.

Berger, M. "Vintage Fords Abandoned Along Side of Highway," Weather.com, www.weather.com/science/news/pat-harvey-vintage-fords-abandoned-20141010, October 2014.

"Hampton Springs Hotel," Desolation Florida, www.desolationflorida.com/2016/04/hampton-springs-hotel.

Wagner, L. "In Final Report, Experts Identify Remains at Notorious Reform School," *NPR*, www.npr.org/sections/thetwo-way/2016/01/21/463846093/in-final-report-experts-identify-remains-at-notorious-reform-school.